Living the Remote Dream
A Guide To Seeing the World, Setting Records, and Advancing Your Career

DARREN MURPH

Foreword by Tim Stevens

Cover design by Brian 'Doc' Reed

DEDICATION

This work is dedicated to my wife, soulmate, and lifelong travel partner, Dana.

To my parents, for instilling the love of wander in me.

To my late Uncle Jr., who understood that life is best lived with a pup by your side.

And to you – here's to whatever adventure awaits.

ABOUT THE AUTHOR

Darren Murph holds a Guinness World Record as the Most Prolific Professional Blogger on Earth. During his career as a writer, reviewer, and editor at *Engadget*, a consumer electronics publication, he published over 22,000 articles using 6.2 million words. He's penned two Apple-focused guides (iPad Secrets and iPhone Secrets, both available through John Wiley & Sons). His work is featured in Gear Patrol, BGR, Popular Science, Mazda's Zoom-Zoom owner's magazine, Oprah.com, Gadling, Thrillist, and ShermansTravel. He has appeared on ABC, PBS, CTV, and NBC television and radio programs.

He holds a B.S. in Business Management from North Carolina State University (Go Pack!), as well as an MBA from Campbell University. He's an author, a storyteller, a project manager, and a consultant. He'll work on anything that's awesome, really.

More important than that, however, is this: he's a husband to the most beautiful photographer in the known universe, and a dad to a French Bulldog / Boston Terrier pup named Gangster. He has driven a motorized vehicle in all 50 U.S. states, and has visited 43 countries to date. His overarching goal is to visit everywhere at least once, and yes, he means *everywhere*. He prefers remote national parks to bustling cities, has a knack for making the most of frequent flyer miles, and believes in the healing powers of southern hospitality. He lives in a tiny town along North Carolina's magnificent Inner Banks, where traffic jams are only triggered by repositioning tractors.

He's also open to consulting with you (*yes, you!*) or speaking at your next event. From coaching to product strategy, he'd love to help. He can be reached at darrenmurph@gmail.com, or @darrenmurph on Twitter. Please, say hello!

CONTENTS

LIVING THE REMOTE DREAM

ACKNOWLEDGMENTS

Much like life itself, the construction of this book was a journey. Writing occurred in airplane seats overlooking the world, on secluded outskirts of National Parks, and on couches of people I'm fortunate to know. It's because of those people – and people I'll never meet again – that this book was seen through to the end.

An unending stream of thanks goes to my wife. She encouraged me to embrace the penning of this guide, never grumbled about the time I sunk into it, and celebrated the completion of every chapter. Everything that I'm able to share in these pages is due to her love for our life together. She's responsible for the sensational imagery on the cover, and for making this book 1,212 percent better with her edits.

I owe heaps of gratitude to Brian 'Doc' Reed for his magnificent design work. Thank you for bestowing your vision, and for having an epic beard.

To my parents, thank you. Thank you for teaching me the value in seeing beyond the place that one calls home, while proving that home will always be the most beautiful place of all.

To my peers, colleagues, editors, and mentors over the years: Thank you for showing me the ropes, grilling me on edits, and challenging me to learn.

To my Creator: Thank you for putting me on such a beautiful planet. Until I've seen every mountain, river, and desert, your artwork will continue to be my drive and inspiration.

To every last soul I've met while wandering through 40-some-odd countries: thank you for showing me the value in embracing a culture other than my own. You're beautiful.

FOREWORD

I've done my time in cubicles. As a software engineer, then architect, then enterprise architect, I cycled the nine-to-five grind for years on end, punching the clock, climbing the corporate ladder, ticking off each and every one of the many and tedious cliches that come along with the prototypical desk job. I earned my own office, which afforded the benefit of a door I could close and music I could listen to without headgear. I was well-paid, well-respected, and well on my way to the upper-echelons of corporate society.

It all felt a bit stale.

I kept sane by writing. Essays, editorials, blog posts, reviews, whatever. I'd be up at 6am to get a few hours in before work, then would spend my evenings and weekends typing away. It was exhausting, managing dual careers, but only by finding time for one could I bear to stick with the other. I loved writing, and I was lucky to be getting paid for it. Eventually, I was lucky enough to get noticed.

It took over a decade of sacrifice to pull it off but I was able to turn my hobby into my career, leaving behind the stable and perpetually lucrative world of software for the tumultuous and consistently threadbare world of journalism. Not the most sound financial decision, perhaps, but I haven't regretted it. Not yet, anyway.

That's not to say that there haven't been some low points -- plenty, as a matter of fact -- but that radical career change opened the door to some amazing opportunities. One of those opportunities was to truly embrace the concept of remote work. Another was an opportunity to become very closely acquainted with one Mr. Darren Murph. It's thanks to those two happenings that I was in turn given another opportunity, that of writing the foreword that you're doing me the great honor of reading.

After leaving behind the software world I became Editor-in-Chief at Engadget, and Darren Managing Editor. This meant leading a virtual team of (amazing) physical individuals scattered all over the globe. I had to get to know them all, I had to learn their goals in life, their career aspirations, their conflicts, their struggles, and all the beautiful information one must gather to be an effective manager. It was hard, really hard, and we were far from perfect, but Darren and I built an incredibly strong team of incredibly diverse individuals. All the while, I was able to work much of the time from my beautiful home in the woods in the middle of nowhere, which is where I quite like to be.

I bring all this up to make a point: It's not just possible to be a great employee from anywhere, it's more than possible to be a great manager from anywhere. The skills you need to inspire people don't require watercoolers and non-mandatory, late-day, semi-social mixers in the cafeteria. Wherever you're working, all that really matters is whether you care about what you're doing and care about those you're doing it with. Sometimes, when you mix in office politics, that message gets a little bit lost.

Now, just a few more words before you dive in, words that are especially important if you are in the unfortunate state of having never met Mr. Murph personally.

First, you should know that Darren Murph is one of the most consistently motivated, highly intense, and overwhelmingly driven individuals on the planet. The phrase "high on life" falls pathetically short of the mark. Most people, if given the opportunity to vacation with Darren Murph, would need a follow-up vacation of equal or greater length to recover. For that reason, if some of the more extreme examples of remote working cited in the following pages feel unrealistic for you, that is fine. It simply means that you, like I, are a mortal human being. Read these moments as something to aspire to, just like reading this has made me more inclined to hurry up and finish my own damned book.

Secondly, you should know that Mr. Murph, being a native North Carolinian, speaks with a bit of a southern accent. Not a good 'ol boy drawl of the Deep South, or the rolling banjo twang of the Mississippi Delta, but a gentle bit of respectfully delivered Appalachian nuance that makes just about whatever it is he's talking about come across with a smile. If you're so inclined, I recommend adding a bit of that flavor to the voice in your head, the one that's reading this very text to you right now. It'll be a more authentic experience that way. I guarantee it.

Enjoy the book. The way you look at work, at life, and at the precarious balance in between is about to change.

-Tim Stevens
 Editor-at-Large, CNET.
@Tim_Stevens

LIVING THE REMOTE DREAM

1. INTRODUCTION

IN four years and nineteen days, I went from never having published a word in my life to claiming a Guinness World Record as the planet's most prolific professional blogger. It was *precisely* as easy as you're envisioning it to be.

"You're *still* on the first article?! You've been at it for, like, five hours now! I haven't heard from you all day and, seriously, you're making 50 cents an hour. This is my nightmare."

That, to the best of my remembrance, is what my fiancé (now wife) conveyed to me over the phone on the evening of July 10, 2006 – the day that my first article[1] for a publication dubbed *Engadget* went live. At the time, we viewed that moment very differently. She saw it as the start of a hopeless hobby that would undoubtedly derail our upcoming nuptials, spoil our honeymoon, and ensure that our life together would be entirely devoid of awesomeness. I recognized that it was my ticket to freedom.

In the years since, both of us were proven right to some degree. There've been times where I haven't spent more than a couple of hours in a day *not* looking at a computer screen, but conversely, we've motored across all 50 U.S. states and have crossed 43 (and counting) international borders together. Travel may not be your thing, but it is ours – point is, we're doing what most folks would save for retirement, but during a time in our life where we're healthy, mobile,

---

[1] Murph, Darren. "Kensington's iPod FM transmitter with RDS." *Engadget.*
<http://www.engadget.com/2006/07/10/kensingtons-ipod-fm-transmitter-with-rds/>

and capable of flying 36 hours in an economy seat without metamorphosing into dust.

Shortly after waking up from the most uncomfortable redeye sleep I've ever experienced, I turned 30. Three decades on Earth, a Guinness World Record in my field of employment, 43 unique passport stamps, the respect of my peers, a passion for experiencing cultures beyond my own, and the realization that one key tenet made all of this possible: aeroelasticity. Just kidding, but only to prove that no rocket science is involved. Plainly, **I'm no longer tied to an office.**

The notion of telecommuting is hardly a novel one. For as long as telephones and the Internet have existed, so has the desire to shed the unspeakable burden of the daily commute. But, as it turns out, saving oneself a few hours per day is only the start.

I've lived an outlandish life. Somehow, I've managed to traverse vast areas of the globe while working more feverishly than most of my contemporaries – even those who devoutly situate themselves in an arbitrary piece of real estate each day.

Logically, this seems impossible. The more one is on the run, the less time one has for accomplishing work… or, so says conventional wisdom. Over the years, I've been asked from time to time how I manage to accomplish so much while living so hard. I've fielded serious inquiries about the art of finding more than 24 hours in a day, but alas, I've yet to fully penetrate the space–time continuum.

In this guide, I'll seek to reveal every secret, hack, and loophole I've found to achieving what many (or, perhaps just me) view as the Holy Grail of experiencing life. It's been said that people usually find themselves with wealth or time, but never both. The wealthy are too busy acquiring wealth to spend any time enjoying life, while those flush with time have no means to spend it in places they yearn to go.

The modern assumption of the workplace has managed to keep a staggering amount of people wrapped up in the system, returning day after day to a cube in a predetermined location. A cube, mind you, where people promptly open up a computer and work for hours on end. A cube where the work that's accomplished is rarely ever tied back to the location of said cube.

I've heard the arguments for "face time," and I recognize the laughable assumption that no employee can be left to his or her own devices and trusted to put forth their best effort. I've witnessed managers refuse to grant any flexibility to an underling's schedule for fear that they themselves would never be granted the same luxury. Put simply, tying one's work to a precise place on the map makes no sense for much of the modern workforce.

I'm oversimplifying to some degree, but recall that we've only made it to the introduction. It's clear that some working scenarios will never be suited for remote work – manufacturing roles, medical researchers, and the prized dentists of the world. (Granted, virtual reality and precision robotics are getting awfully close to enabling cavities in Timbuktu to be addressed from Honolulu.) For those roles and the people called to occupy them, my advice probably won't hit home. But for those who already work in a knowledge industry, or those who'd love nothing more than to change paths and land a career where location matters not, the chapters to come are written for you.

Tens of millions of people show up to locales each day to engage in work that fulfills them. Indeed, I'm eternally grateful to physicians, professors, bankers, janitors, athletes, and SportsCenter anchors for showing up and making life a little better for me. If you're engaged with your career in a way that gives you tremendous purpose, hold onto that. If you're happy to interact with and shape the lives of people you see when going into work each day, hold onto that. If you're flustered with your role and are longing for something more, transitioning to a remote position is an alternative to training for a different career altogether. Said another way, if you aren't able to build a legacy at your current job, a role where location is of no concern just might be your solution.

It's worth pointing out that operating as I do isn't always as marvelous as it may seem. The glitz and glamor of never-ending travel, or simply spending an unusual amount of time in places other than an office, is wrought with challenges. What you see of a remote worker through Instagram shots and Facebook updates doesn't tell their whole story. Awkward sleep schedules, addressing client needs at all hours of the night, a feeling of constant connectedness, and a perpetual hunt for a solid Internet connection all are commonplace.

But still, it's worth it.

Sinking your teeth into a career that enables remote work is no magic bullet. I still haven't figured out how to get rich quickly. I still can't embrace transatlantic cruises for fear of being without an Internet signal for more than 24 hours. My so-called work/life balance is thoroughly *out* of balance – in the end, I've decided to choose **life**. Even if it means working exceptionally hard for it, at least I'm choosing where the work happens. So, too, can you.

2. RECORD-SETTING FOCUS

Focus and efficiency. Two terms that you've probably heard bandied about in commercials for sports drinks, and two terms that seem to always come up in motivational speeches. Unfortunately, they've become somewhat watered down over the years, unable to elicit the same sort of visceral response that a coach or mentor would hope. Perhaps it's because the definition of these two words tends to be laid out in relative terms. Telling a hyperconnected teenager to focus on an examination may be the same as asking him or her to simply put their smartphone in Airplane Mode for an hour. Telling a pilot that's about to land in an area with low visibility to focus will probably lead to a much different reaction.

So, with that said, I'll attempt to explain how focus and efficiency have enabled me to work remotely, and indeed, have helped me accomplish even more than I would have if confined to an office.

A variety of studies[2] have proven that people are more effective and more efficient when they're left to focus on a task for **long, uninterrupted periods of time**. That finding is at the heart of doing well remotely, and it also happens to be the reason that work suffers when chained to an office. In a typical office setting, workers are surrounded by noise and incessant disruptions. Just "popping in" to

---

[2]Desmarais, Christina. "5 TED Talks to Help You Work Smarter."*Inc.*<http://www.inc.com/christina-desmarais/5-ted-talks-that-can-help-you-work-smarter.html>

one's office not only breaks concentration, but it derails whatever task was being worked on for an unknowable amount of time. In U.S. culture, it's considered rude or haughty to close one's office door, when in fact, it should be embraced. Most of those drive-by distractions result in little to no important momentum, and they most certainly halt whatever mental processes were churning prior. The drive-by, much like the unscheduled phone call, is catastrophically disruptive to work efficiency. For as annoying as an incessant stream of emails can become, at least email provides the owner with the ability to respond on their own time. That difference allows remote workers to focus intensely on completing a task or series of tasks without any breaks in focus. When the project is complete, those emails are silently waiting. Extrapolate this throughout an entire workday, workweek, or year, and the results can be impressive.

Not only are you able to accomplish more in less time, but you're able to jump to the next task much more quickly than those in the office. While office chatter is ongoing, you're diving into another initiative. While Mike is dropping by Tom's office to speak a little about work and a little about the weekend, you're motoring through a task that no one expected to be complete until next month. When you're left to build your own office, you're able to choose your distractions. If you need a quick jog with your pup to clear your head after working through a complex problem for two straight hours, you can. But there's a gigantic difference between an individual controlling what interruptions enter their day and working in an environment where disruptions can (and often do) happen continually.

Roughly, I estimate that eight normal hours in a typical office setting only nets you around six workable hours. And even those hours aren't engineered for maximum efficiency. We've all been that guy or gal on the phone listening intently for an important message from someone on the other end, quick to wave the index finger in the face of anyone who dares interrupt. Why is that? Because it's possible to learn more, to hear more, to compute more, and to deliver more when you're able to sink deep into your own groove. How effective would your sleep be if you had someone "dropping in" every 45 minutes? Something tells me that parents currently raising a new bundle of joy would have a pretty exact answer to that.

For me, I do everything possible to control my working

environment. At times, I'm hunkered down in my home office with my phone switched off. Other times, I'm in a cramped 757, frantically pecking away as if I'm a T-Rex – replete with tiny arms and a huge head – being smashed by the reclined seat in front of me. Every now and again, I'm on the back porch of an overwater bungalow. The reason this works is my **appreciation for time**. In an office, you're stuck there for eight hours regardless of whether you actually have eight hours of things you can accomplish. When *you* pick the office, it behooves you to utterly demolish any work that stands between you and whatever you want to do next. When the possibilities are this endless, you're in a perpetual state of heightened awareness. You're aware that it benefits you to accomplish your work in the most effective, efficient manner possible. You're aware that by focusing entirely on the task at hand, the reward will be time to spend on something else – sometimes, that's simply another work-related task, but even in those instances, you're still doing yourself a favor. You're aware that any disruption that you haven't chosen yourself is altogether unacceptable, which is something that many in an office are never positioned to recognize.

Regrettably, improving your focus and efficiency isn't something that occurs overnight. The upside, however, is that your potential focus and efficiency gains are next to limitless.

For those unaware, *Engadget* is an online media property that covers the wide world of consumer electronics. It's where talented, frenetic, passionate writers go to write about gizmos, software, and the global impact of technology. If that still reads like Russian to you, chew on this: You know those writers at *The New York Times* that specifically cover baseball? As in, they attend games, score interviews with players and coaches, and then write about all-things-baseball in the paper that ends up in your mailbox? That's what I did, except my baseball was gadgetry, and my paper was the Internet.

I spent over seven years there, and outside of a six week sabbatical in early 2012, I never took a proper day of vacation. I may have claimed a few days as vacation, but in practice, my mind was never switched off. In many cases, I'd enjoy the spoils of daylight – those hours were ideal for hiking and visiting new places during business hours – while devoting myself to work during evenings and early mornings. Still, in that period, I meandered through glorious valleys in Joshua Tree National Park, jumped from the towering cliffs of Hawaii into the Pacific Ocean, drove through 300 miles of dust to find the northernmost land border crossing between the U.S. and Canada, relaxed in hot springs while visiting both Taiwan and Costa Rica, and filled a 26 page passport to capacity. (I've since obtained a 52 pager, which I'd highly recommend to those that'll be applying for a new one in the near future.)

At its largest, *Engadget* employed nearly 30 writers, reporters, and perennial pranksters from across the globe. We were a remote team, with self-starting individuals positioned in Oakland, Tokyo, the outskirts of London, an island in the Philippines, Staten Island, Michigan, France, Spain, Amsterdam, and Canada. (Proving the stereotypes correct, those Canadians were *definitely* the nicest of the bunch.)

When asked to step in as Managing Editor, I did so for the privilege of working alongside Tim Stevens, my Editor-in-Chief. He, too, operated remotely from the woods of New York, traveling as required to make this operation tick. The tasks were huge. We had to hire dozens of new writers, train them to be the best in the industry, and manage an unending stream of pertinent questions from employees in just about every time zone imaginable. Oh, and we had to continue to write – *Engadget*'s readers expected between 40 and 50 articles per day to grace the site's pages, and those articles certainly weren't going to pen themselves. The perpetual pressure of maintaining a news organization that is expected to be in top form literally every hour of every single day is unlike anything else I've ever experienced. It's exhilarating and exhausting; comically demanding and tragically relentless. The kind of place where a 20 minute hiccup in the day could lead your property to be second – an unforgiveable thing, mind you – in breaking a story.

All the while, however, my gratitude never wavered. The pressure drove me to find the most efficient and effective methods to work. I was made *better* because I was allowed to work remotely, and I saw that same magic happen in every single person that Tim and I hired. We gave meaningful employment to people in places like rural Utah, North Carolina, and Idaho – people who had searched in futility for well-paying, rewarding roles in locations that they cherished. We brought the work to them, right where they stood, and they poured *everything* that they had into making our publication better.

For employers reading along, it's important to note that enabling a remote infrastructure is about so much more than simply allowing a worker to have more flexibility. Remote roles enable entire families to remain together. They enable tiny communities to hold tight to ones that remain there. They enable a broader distribution of wealth and opportunity, allowing our world as a whole to become incrementally more stable with every hire.

Every remote worker that I've ever employed has worked absurdly hard to express their thanks for the opportunity. Hiring a remote worker isn't an excuse to hang a millstone around their neck – based on what I've seen, it's not even necessary. Those given the autonomy to create and deliver on their own terms rarely forget how great they have it. The character and passion found in remote workers is second to none, and I'm a firm believer that any organization could benefit from having more passionate people in its ranks.

Even when the demands of *Engadget* were forcing me to lose sleep, ignore my family, and pushing me terrifyingly close to the brink of depression – potential pitfalls of any job in any location, mind you – those around me made it impossible to leave. So long as Tim Stevens was pouring his heart and soul into the site for 18 hours per day, so too would I. So long as my comrades from outposts around the planet were writing as hard as they could, so too would I. These periods of extreme overwork were made easier by the ability to overwork myself from anywhere. As I'll point out later, the remote dream is oftentimes *un*dreamy. When your office is anywhere, it's occasionally not practical to leave. Those downsides are worth taking on for the chance to work alongside others that'll pull you through and get you back to enjoying more of what matters, but they're no less authentic or unavoidable.

Now that we're on the same page, I want to make clear that I wasn't always efficient at writing. When I began as an *Engadget* freelancer in July of 2006, my first article took around five hours to complete. During that time, I took a shot at writing what I thought was a solid story, and then my editor (the inimitable Ryan Block, to whom I owe heaps of gratitude) tore me and my story to pieces. We fought back and forth for a while, and eventually, an article that was largely written by Ryan was allowed to be published for all to see. Said in the most efficient way I know: Five hours to write roughly 250 words is inefficient.

Over the course of the next four years, I improved considerably. I became so adept at writing about technology, and so captivated by the chase of writing more than I did the day before, that I eventually earned a Guinness World Record for my work. During a four year span between the summers of 2006 and 2010, I wrote more than any other professional blogger in the universe. My dear colleague Chris Ziegler[3] encouraged me to apply for the record, and the team at Guinness World Records spent a number of months (unsuccessfully) trying to disprove my claims. Eventually, a plaque arrived from London, officially ushering me into the record book[4]. My career at *Engadget* continued through October of 2013[5], where the count reached well over 22,000, and the word total soared beyond the 6 million mark.

When people ask me about the accomplishment, I tell them that I have a world record in efficiency. It's not like I was born to write. I studied business in school, and thoroughly detested every English course I was ever forced to take. What I figured out was the method to staying focused, and using that focus to help me achieve my goals. **During that record-setting window, my *Engadget* post count averaged out to one article published every two hours, 24/7/365, for four straight years. That includes weekends, holidays, and days that I spent visiting all 50 states in the nation that I call home, along with over 30 countries.**

I say that to point out that I did a lot more than work. I traveled – traveled like a madman – and I saw things that I'd only ever dreamt of seeing. I met people from far-flung islands, soaked up cultures different than my own, and used all of that as continual motivation to make myself even more efficient as a writer.

---

[3]Ziegler, Chris. *Twitter.* <https://twitter.com/zpower>

[4]Guinness World Records. "Most prolific professional blogger." <http://www.guinnessworldrecords.com/world-records/most-prolific-professional-blogger/>

[5]Murph, Darren. "Farewell, and thank you." *Engadget.*<http://www.engadget.com/2013/10/15/farewell-and-thank-you/>

I committed to learning a new word each day. I made a point to watch television and pay attention to comedic references that I could riff off of. I read everything I could get my eyes on from writers that I knew were superior to me in terms of skill and style. And I was determined to be faster, better, and stronger at my job, if only to give myself more time to truly live when I wasn't on the proverbial clock.

To do this, I had to become something of a monster when I was working. I was passionate about what I did, and equally passionate about doing it quickly. When I was in the middle of an article, my wife knew that interrupting me would severely disrupt my flow. She understood that I'd appreciate reserving any distractions for emergencies, and I'll readily concede that having such an arrangement was beneficial for my focus and efficiency. To achieve maximum gains, you're going to have to change your lifestyle. You're going to have to draw new lines in the sand, and you're going to have to make some things that were previously acceptable, unacceptable. The same could be said for someone looking to achieve gains in fitness – this isn't a one-time tweak, but a commitment to devoting yourself entirely to work each day for the windows that you choose.

I'll also take this opportunity to point out just how critical it is to find work that you love – work that you're truly and unashamedly passionate about. A dear friend of mine, Tynan, has written a guide to mastering habits. (It's titled Superhuman By Habit[6], and you should totally buy it.) According to his logic, creating habits enables you to churn through tasks with minimal effort, as there's no need for willpower to complete a habit.

The same can be said for work that you adore. If you're exhausting all of your available willpower each day just to get through the tasks you're paid to do, you aren't apt to ever achieve peak efficiency. However, if you're engaged with work on a level where you're motivated to create habits, you'll position yourself to achieve peak efficiency.

---

[6]Tynan. "Superhuman By Habit." *Amazon.*<http://www.amazon.com/Superhuman-Habit-Becoming-Possible-Yourself/dp/1503295591>

Life is entirely too short to stay stuck in a job that you aren'tat least *happy* with. We live in a universe where creative people in rural towns with minimal capital can sell their wares to others all over the globe. Barriers to success have never been more penetrable. It's easy to roll one's eyes here, I know, but I'd urge you to not just brush this recommendation aside. If you aren't in a role where you're able to focus on doing your best work due to an ingrained dissatisfaction, evaluate why. Perhaps you just need an attitude adjustment, or perhaps you need to take a chance and embrace an opportunity elsewhere. Whatever the case, do something – *anything* – and see if it puts you in a better place to become more focused and more efficient.

In early 2008, I was crammed in a room with a dozen or so other editors from *Engadget*. The scene was Las Vegas, and the event was the Consumer Electronics Show. It's simply not possible for me to explain the importance of this single show to anyone who doesn't work in the media, but I'll try. Our entire year was made in this week. Millions upon millions of new readers would visit our pages during these seven days to read up on the most exiting and promising gadgetry that would be announced at CES. It was our duty to cover those announcements – hundreds of them – in real-time.

As a freelancer at the time, I was paid for each article I published. An uncomplicated arrangement, to be certain. It was also around that time that I realized just how beneficial it'd be if I were able to write a truly absurd amount of content in a laughably short amount of time. After all, it was CES, and there were *plenty* of stories to write.

I'll be frank: the allure of a hefty payday and the chance to do something that had never been done before were substantial motivators. In a single 24 hour period, I published 58 articles. To this day, that record stands at the site, and I still look back and chuckle about how much I stashed in my retirement account on that one *painfully* tiring day. Around a year later, I was summarily told that I'd either be capped on earnings, or that I could join the company as a salaried employee. I was working so hard, so fast, that I was effectively mangling the budget. What an honor.

In all seriousness, everyone will have slightly different triggers to becoming focused and efficient, but finding them is critical to doing more with less effort.

I'll close this chapter by talking about politics. Specifically, office politics. In some instances, I've heard that shutting out unnecessary distractions at work in order to be more productive leads to an unbecoming image. In other words, those who aren't receptive to chitchatting and engaging in absurdly unproductive office shenanigans are frowned upon, passed over for promotions, and generally disliked. Which isn't false. This is absolutely the case at far too many organizations, where one's perception is valued more highly than one's contributions.

To this I say: **leave**. If the above describes your work environment, your company is doomed. It may not fail this year or even the next, but a company that focuses on perception over production will eventually falter. There's a term for the opposite of this, and it's called meritocracy. Remote-based employees do best when they operate within a company that looks first at someone's merit, and second at everything else. A company that realizes a quiet employee isn't a jerk, but in fact a productive asset, is a company that you want to work for. Moreover, it's the kind of company that's going to be around for the long haul.

Face time is still important, and on remote teams, those rare moments where everyone is in the same place take on enhanced meaning. At *Engadget*, we made a point to gather as many of us as possible for a week each summer. For a few short days, we'd crowd into some mesmerizingly large house on Long Island or Maine or Montreal, and we'd reconnect. We'd work together, we'd plan together, and we'd scheme together. We'd catch up, we'd darn near kill each other on go-karts, and we'd bond like no other team on Earth. *This* is the office worth going into – one designed to bring souls closer together, not to exhaust each other.

In business, results matter. You should make it a goal to align yourself with a firm (or start your own!) that recognizes this. Not only will it make it easier to focus on being efficient (instead of being a member of the in-crowd), but you'll find yourself far happier in the long run. An easy way to tell whether or not you're in a place that values production over all else is to ask yourself this: if you closed a deal over email just before heading out to hike in Hawaii, would your colleagues marvel at your ability to intermix business and pleasure, or would they stew and grumble over the fact that you're in Hawaii? Merit-focused companies are ran by real humans – humans that enjoy chitchat and love to have fun – but they operate in a culture that appreciates quiet introspection, intense focus, and maximum efficiency. They care about doing great work when it's time to work, and moving on to enjoy life when it's time to live. Find that, and you'll find something worth focusing on.

3. NONLINEAR WORKDAY

Routines are important – vital, even. They keep you sane, they keep you grounded, and they provide some level of normalcy that makes it a lot easier to churn through work. Routines are safe, familiar, and beneficial, but only when you're the one dictating the particulars. For those who have to clock in and clock out at the same time each day, the routine is dictated for you. You're forced to either rise earlier than necessary or to sit in seemingly unending traffic. You're forced to either stay past dinner or, again, sit in seemingly unending traffic. And for what?

When you're manufacturing items and attempting to meet a certain goal in a certain window of time, specific shifts make sense. In many cases, they're simply unavoidable. But in other areas of the working world, work continues to be accomplished between 9AM and 5PM simply because we're too lazy to do anything about it. Arriving at 2:51PM for a flight that departs at 2:50PM causes severe disruption. But responding to an email asking for your input on a new strategy shouldn't posses the same level of time sensitivity.

Beyond all of that, what's most galling about the typical "9 to 5" mentality is just how many hours this leaves on the table. There aren't many economies left in the world that aren't global on some level. Schedules that were determined scores ago didn't take time zones into account. They didn't take the Internet into account. They didn't take voicemail and inboxes and notifications and mobility into account. It's time we started accounting for all of that.

My brain aches just considering how many man hours are lost – let alone how many wills are broken – by the unwritten rule of 9 to 5. By shoving that many people onto subways, highways, and airplanes just to work during a set of hours that were drawn up eons ago, we're losing efficiency on a gargantuan scale. The people that are sitting in traffic on both sides of their workday are not able to be productive. Their souls are being brutalized by unnecessarily long hauls to and from their families. And no one is stopping to point out that the work they accomplished from 9 to 5 could've been done from 3 to 11 or 12 to 8 or any combination of the above.

Granted, this wouldn't *always* work, but that's not the point. The point is that 9 to 5 doesn't *always* work, either. In my own life, embracing a nonlinear workday with a handful of predetermined routines has enabled me to accomplish more, waste less time, enjoy the perks of traveling during nonpeak periods, and be more available for things that truly matter.

Allow me to describe an honest-to-goodness example of how a nonlinear workday transpires. The clock strikes midnight on Monday, and I hit the hay in a rental cabin in Columbia Falls, Montana. I sleep for eight solid hours, waking up at 8AM – correction, I *attempt* to wake at 8AM, but actually rise around 8:15AM, with nary a worry in the world over those 15 minutes. I put on a pot of coffee, flip on one of my favorite radio programs, and open my computer. For the next 1.5 hours I plow through emails, finish up a project from the evening prior, and return a phone call that I missed. Now that my blood is sufficiently pumping, I throw on a different set of clothing and push through a one-hour workout. I walk one room over and shower, walk two rooms over and cook myself brunch, and then sit down for another half-hour of work.

It's around 11:45AM. I've enjoyed a quiet cup of coffee, I'm caught up with work, my daily exercise routine is in the books, and I've prepared my own meal using ingredients that I selected. Let's look at what I *haven't* done: spent a half-hour putting on a wardrobe that society says I have to wear when heading to an office; grabbed some breakfast bar filled with heaven knows what; spent even one single minute in traffic; parted ways with even a penny in fuel; cursed out some other overburdened idiot who ought to have his license revoked. So far, so good!

Next, I toss a few heavy layers on, crank up the car, and drive 30 minutes to a giant mountain with tons of snow and empty ski lifts. I proceed to enjoy four solid hours of skiing at Whitefish Mountain Resort, where my body is able to do something other than sit idly in a desk chair and my mind is able to wander. At some point during the day, a few creative solutions come to mind for issues that have been bugging me. Solutions, mind you, that would never have surfaced had I not made a conscious choice to get outside, enjoy the fresh air, and break away from the grind.

At 4PM, I head back, suffering through the kind of free-flowing traffic that rush hour drivers have only dreamt about. By 4:45PM, I'm hard at work, catching up on what I've missed and pressing ahead on a few longer projects. Two hours later, I break for a dinner that I'm able to prepare myself – yet another mental stimulation that's remarkably rewarding. By 8PM, I'm settling down to watch a couple of NBA games on the 'tube while accomplishing massive strides at work, still wonderfully peddling at this hour, enabling me to do hours in a busy office.

This is just one day, just one small example of how a nonlinear workday happens. If you were to ask me about this particular day in a year, all I'd remember was the amazing weather at Whitefish and just how few people were crowding the slopes on a Tuesday. But, as it turns out, I worked a full shift on that particular day. I made huge gains at work. I made myself proud, aided my colleagues, and moved my company forward. I also treated my soul, my mind, and my stomach. It was a full day. Full of work, and full of enjoyment.

As you can probably imagine, having a nonlinear workday is even more impressive when you factor partial vacation days in. This type of working scenario allows highly dedicated employees to make their PTO days stretch for much longer. Some will want to truly *get away*, which is entirely understandable. Even on days where you need to put in a full day's worth of work, constructing them in a nonlinear way enables you to make so much more of each 24 hours that you're blessed with.

Let's take the above example and see what would've happened had I not pushed for a remote role, and if I had to work the usual 9 to 5 shift. For starters, I would've been wading through a large city, not picturesque Montana, so the rest of my explanation is essentially null and void. Nevertheless, I'll proceed. The aforementioned ski resort closes each day at 4PM, which means that it would be impossible to ever enjoy the mountain on any day where I was working. Thirdly, I would've been forced to deal with rush hour commutes on both ends of my workday, stealing an extra hour or so from me that I wouldn't get to spend on exercise, cooking, personal projects, reading, or whatever else. You get the point.

Even I'll confess that not every nonlinear workday works out as swimmingly as the ski day mentioned above. Sometimes, you have an unavoidable conference call in the middle of the day. Occasionally, you have to be online at a specific moment in time to ensure that a launch goes smoothly. In general, however, you'll give yourself many, many more chances to truly enjoy life if you're willing to work at atypical hours. Yes, it requires a lot more focus (something I'll devote an entire chapter to in the pages to come), and it works best when operating on a team that relies less on rigidly scheduled meetings and more on ongoing conversations carried out over email, IM, or any number of collaborative tools (Slack[7], I'm looking at you).

I've had hundreds of workdays that are more exciting, more joyous, and more adventurous than the vacation days of those cramped in offices. I don't say that to brag; in fact, being able to admit that is tremendously disheartening. I've been fortunate to work in roles where nonlinear workdays are accepted, and I wish that more people would embrace it. In so many cases, it matters not (or exceedingly little) when a reply happens within a 24 hour window. So long as you're keeping a daily check on your work duties, and you're being diligent about making progress, your colleagues aren't apt to care whether you work from 6 to 8 or 10 to 12 or during any other two-hour chunk of time.

I've seen 98 percent of what there is to see in Kuala Lumpur in just 36 manic hours. I've flown on 9-hour redeye flights just so I wouldn't have to take vacation time to get from Point A to Point B. I've volunteered to work 60+ hours in a week covering a trade show so I'd have a justifiable reason to be somewhere awesome. What's possible with nonlinear workdays is limited only by your imagination, your tolerance for uneven sleep schedules, and your willingness to accept volatility.

Even in roles where you can develop these atypical routines, it's

---

[7] Slack. <https://slack.com/>

simply not possible for everything to always pan out. I've had vacation days wholly consumed by Skype calls during a work crisis. I've had to miss an event that I had a nontransferable ticket to because an important meeting (as in, not just *any* meeting) was rescheduled. These realities of the volatile work world ensure that kinks will be thrown into even the most thoughtfully planned day, but it makes those days where everything works out that much sweeter. I'd much rather carve a little fun into the occasional workday than to live in a world where weekends and a few PTO blocks were all I had to look forward to. If the ride gets a little bumpy, so be it.

4. THE BUCKET LIST

Conventional wisdom would have you believe a couple of things about the so-called bucket list. First, that it's not actually a thing. When most folks consider a bucket list, they do so only after hearing that someone else went somewhere awesome. Like this: "Oh! You just got back from Kauai?! That's a place for the bucket list!" Then, predictably, that sentence is followed by one's mind heading elsewhere as to not focus on the fact that they don't actually *have* a bucket list. The second is far more subtle. While it's not written in stone, most folks are conditioned to believe that "bucket list" actually means "after retirement list." It's time we did something about that.

One of the best things I've ever done was create a bucket list – an actual, bona fide list of places I yearn to visit and things I long to do. My wife and I sat down shortly after our honeymoon and wrote down a long, meandering list of places that we'd love to see. At the time, I was over the moon after having visited the Big Island of Hawaii for the first time. I'd been blessed to travel as a child, but never to somewhere like Hawaii. That place was pure magic. It was also the only place I was going to visit the entire year, since I'd just plowed through every vacation day I had and was expected back in the office upon my return.

That abrupt reentry into the office was the beginning of the end. My first real role out of university was a conventional office job, but I didn't hang around for long. I was tremendously appreciative for the chance to escape reality for a fortnight, but internally, I wanted more. My soul *needed* more. I didn't mind working hard, but I had a feeling that I ought to be working smart. If you, like me, find yourself in a job where your primary objectives are completed via a telephone and a computer, it's time to take this whole "bucket list" thing a lot more seriously.

By their nature, remote roles usually involve more travel than other jobs. While certain objectives can be accomplished using email, phone, and videoconferencing, others will demand that you be at various places throughout the year. Perhaps it's a trade show, or a conference, or an offsite team retreat. If you end up in a position where this is your reality, embrace it. While at *Engadget*, I was tasked to cover a number of events around the globe on behalf of the company. It was strenuous work – the planning and execution had to be perfect, as my time at the event was limited and it was largely on me to ensure that everything went smoothly. But it enabled me to land in cities and countries that I probably wouldn't visit otherwise.

A few years back, work took me to Germany for a conference. Which was awesome, because visiting Germany was undoubtedly something I wanted to do at some point in my life. But when you're driven by a bucket list, simply visiting one place triggers all sorts of other questions:

- What's nearby? Any national parks, world heritage sites, or can't-miss-monuments?
- Can I carve out time on evenings or weekends to visit another country by train?
- Could I fly into Germany and return home via some other airport?
- How many days could I spend exploring before and after the conference?
- Is there a U2 show going on in Belgium a day after the conference ends?

"Wait, *what?*" That's my wife speaking, by the way, simultaneously baffled and curious about the seriousness of that last inquiry. As it turns out, there *was* a U2 show happening nearby while I was in Germany – all I needed to do was spring for rail passes into Brussels, secure a couple of tickets to the event, and brush up on one of three possible languages that I'd hear that evening. Challenging? Yes. But doable? Oh, totally.

You see, I'm driven by an urge to make the most of every situation I'm given, and in the case of a U2 show in Brussels, I surmised that it'd be more economical to bolt that onto a work trip I was already taking than to try and see one of their other shows closer to home. Plus, I had no issue working from Belgium the following day – if that's the price I have to pay to see U2 in Europe, consider it done.

After the doors were closed on the final day of Photokina, a camera gala in Cologne, my wife and I bolted to Köln Hauptbahnhof. (That's a fancy name for the central rail station, as I understand it.) We joined a train full of mirthful Germans, halfway believing that we'd end up in Brussels and halfway worried that we were heading somewhere else entirely. Worst case scenario? We'd visit a new place in Europe, so, hooray! Plus, I was soothed by the realization that most of my car mates were sober. A year prior, I boarded a train between Hanover and Munich during Oktoberfest, which offered up no overhead storage (it was all filled with kegs of various descriptions) and only one open seat. A seat beside a grown, bearded beast of a man who *loved* the fact that I couldn't understand a single word of whatever anthem these folks were belting out. But, I digress….

That evening, we did indeed make it into one of the most crowded, multilingual venues I've ever had the pleasure of invading. U2 was larger than life, and every so often, I'd remind myself that I was standing in a ~~soccer~~ football stadium in a foreign country listening to U2. Surreal, insane, and *awesome*. Following the encore, the masses poured back into the streets, and my wife and I made a beeline to the same metro stop that we'd arrived into… only to find it blockaded and deserted. By that point, even the heavens were weeping, which is to say that an awful lot of Belgians (and two dazed Americans) were quickly becoming drenched from rainfall. I had no idea what was being said around me, and I certainly couldn't understand why a major metro line in the unofficial capital of the European Union was out of order. As it turns out, neither could the locals.

I was part of a riot for the first time in my adult life. As things transpired, my wife and I ended up befriending a local that spoke English, and he helped navigate us to a secondary metro system that was indeed functional. He proceeded to explain to us that the local newspaper had published a scathing critique of the Brussels metro earlier in the day, and that metro employees had taken the evening don't have to return to an office, you can extend business excursions a bit in either direction and work from a locale that's new and invigorating. Sure, it's still work, but it's also a subsidized ticket to explore. It's all about perspective, you know?

For a few years running, I was able to travel to Tokyo each fall to report on a futuristic trade show dubbed CEATEC. Visiting Tokyo is marvelous, of course, but it becomes even more so when you see where it's positioned on a map. It dawned on me that I could more easily visit the ancient streets of Kyoto if I simply flew into Osaka rather than Tokyo, and then grab a series of trains heading east. I came to cover an electronics jamboree, but ended up also seeing the shrines used in the filming of *Memoirs of a Geisha*. Rather than flying straight home, I took the scenic route – first, a flight from Tokyo to Auckland, where I knocked on the door of Bilbo Baggins' house in central New Zealand, and then onto Tahiti. Mind you, I saw all of this while taking just one or two days of vacation time. The time zone factor enabled me to enjoy plenty of glorious sunshine during the day tiptoeing through Middle Earth, while I clamped down on work duties in the evening and early morning. Make no mistake – I was categorically exhausted – but when your job is the very thing that's enabling you to explore the world, barreling through is no issue at all.

Even if you don't have an innate love for travel, you have an innate love for *something*. The creation of a bucket list does something for motivation that I've yet to see matched by any other singular item. There's something endearing about the process of writing down monuments you'd like to take a selfie with, locations you'd like to leave a piece of your heart in, and outlandish experiences that you'd love to embrace while you're still mobile. Bucket lists don't write themselves. They require quiet introspection, careful deliberation, and purposeful intent. You'll never see two bucket lists that look the same. It's a list that's uniquely you – I'd argue that this list more accurately defines you than your hometown, hobbies, or resume.

It's also worth addressing just how possible it is to operate while being out of an office – or, in fact, out of your usual element. In 2012, my wife and I awoke in a 10' x 10' hut on the southern coast of Upolu, Samoa. We unzipped the mosquito net, walked through 50 yards of sand to reach a shared bathroom, and convinced ourselves that the cold shower we were about to endure was totally worth it. There was no TV, no underground plumbing, and nary a drop of hot water.

Minutes later, a notification popped up on my phone. It was an email from our realtor, who was approximately 7,034 miles away, holding two offers on our home. "Please call me if possible," she wrote, "these expire in 24 hours!". Ecstatic to have finally found a buyer (two, even!), I began pecking away on a reply. The connection wasn't strong enough to maintain a call, so instructions over email would have to suffice. Halfway through the note, another notification – the bucket of mobile data I'd purchased when landing on the island had been used up, and my connection was dead. Poof. Over.

My wife and I had grand plans for that day. We had a national park to visit and a waterfall to swim under. Instead, we flung ourselves into a battered Suzuki and made the two hour trek to "town." From there, I waited an hour to reload my SIM card with data, at which point I was able to send the email I'd tried to send half a day earlier: "I don't want to lose the sale. If it all starts falling apart, I'll take the higher offer as it stands."

We sold the house, and we did eventually make it to see that park and swim under that waterfall.

Just as goals are critical in maintaining momentum in the workplace, a bucket list is a wonderful tool for keeping you focused on what really matters. If you're in the early stages of reevaluating your work situation, the creation of a bucket list will undoubtedly motivate you to find a more flexible role. If you're already in a remote role, a bucket list will serve as a reminder of what you have no excuse to be missing out on.

There's no perfect way to create, execute on, and update a bucket list. Mine began with around 20 locations, and has grown to nearly 50. My wife and I joke that each time we mark a location off, two more are tacked on. But, really, isn't that what a bucket list should be? It shouldn't be a static, inflexible string of bullets. It should be a pulsing, energizing script to a movie called life. Creating these with friends, spouses, partners, and children is even more rewarding. Since there's no limit to how long a bucket list can be, everyone's ambitions can be jotted down. To make it worthwhile, however, you need to reference the list on a regular basis.

I'd suggest a reminder every three months. If you're creating quarterly checkpoints as it pertains to career progress, why not take the opportunity to see how you're doing on your personal objectives, too? There's no better feeling than carving out a weekend to see a place you've always wanted to visit, and having a bucket list has single-handedly improved my planning skills. I've managed to squeeze bucket list visits between job duties, but only because I've kept an eye on the weeks and months ahead. I guess you could say that having a bucket list makes you a better planner, which in turn makes you a better human, which in turn makes those without a bucket list decidedly less awesome. Just kidding. (Sort of.)

It's also important to start checking items off of your list as early as possible. 40+ hours of travel in coach is relatively easy when you're 25. I've heard that it's a lot more difficult when you're 60. Life rarely gets easier as you age. Mobility becomes an issue, sickness becomes an issue, and in general, it's easier to make excuses to stay put as the years tick away. It's also dangerous to stay put for too long. If you look up and two years have flown by without you making time for yourself, it won't feel at all unnatural to hold steady for another decade. If you devote yourself to making travel happen – to *making* time for those things that you wrote down however many years ago –

it'll feel quite strange to not have a trip on the books.

I fly a lot more than the average gent, sure, but if I have a two month runway with nary a flight on the schedule, that triggers an alert in my brain. Suddenly, I'm asking why. I'm opening up my calendar and trying to find a block of days where I can go explore. Just the process of the everlasting chase is so rewarding. Every day is an opportunity to do something you've never done before, or visit a place that you've never been before. It's a chance to meet people you've never met before, a chance to interact with a language you've never spoken before, and a chance to knock off a task at work from a place that most would find unbelievable.

If you're all about the *idea* of travel, but don't exactly have the *means* to travel, all hope isn't lost. There's an art to managing and utilizing points and miles – alternative currencies that airlines and hotels hand out for things like loyalty and signing up for the right credit card. I won't bore you with the details, but I estimate that I've enjoyed upwards of $50,000 worth of free travel in under a decade by knowing how to exploit points and miles. Naturally, having an exceptionally flexible schedule helps me to avoid blackout dates, but considering that I'm here to preach the benefits of remote employment… well, here's another perk!

The easiest way to accumulate miles is to sign up for the right cards (responsibly, of course), fly the same airline month after month, stay at the same hotel chain, and work in a job that requires travel. Frequent business travel can lead to frequent leisure travel.

All of this dreamy talk does require a couple of things, though: time and availability. Two things that are best secured when working in a remote role. While everyone has duties on the home front, only a remote worker can rent an apartment on the Oregon coast for a month to get a taste of saltwater life. Only a remote worker can clock in from a duplex in Key West during the winter and a rental flat in Ireland during the summer. When you take the daily location requirement away from one's job responsibility, you're suddenly positioned to dominate a bucket list while you're still young.

Because of my ongoing flexibility, I've established an automated process whereby I'm emailed immediately should an airfare sale pop up out of the airports closest to me. In 2010, one such notification came in. "Fare sale to Central America!," it read. I paused, collected my emotions, and realized that there was but one unplanned week left in the calendar year. A few clicks later, my wife and I had tickets to Panama. I had no intention to take vacation, and no means to go down there and spend a fortune. So, I Googled around and found someone willing to rent out their condo for a week for less than I've paid to stay in Manhattan for *a night*. A sofabed, a small kitchen, and free Wi-Fi. Sold. That week, I rose at 4:30AM each day to conquer a half day's worth of work, and then I'd put the other half in after sunset. It was a total blur, but between work sessions I managed to zipline through a jungle, walk for miles on untouched beaches, witness a ship full of automobiles cross through the Panama Canal, and visit yet another Hard Rock Café. (For those who don't know me, I've collected over 70 glasses from various Hard Rock Café locations around the globe. It's become "a thing.")

In case it's not obvious, there's a **benefit to the employer** here as well. In my case, an unending desire to achieve items on my bucket list drives me to work harder to keep the role that I've been fortunate enough to fill. The more places I visit, the more I'm inclined to bear down in the workplace. The more flexibility I'm given, the more I'm determined to give back. For employers who may be reading this, I'd urge you to take note: your most ambitious, creative, and productive employees may indeed be the same ones that seem to never be working at all. When you're able to work in a place that suits you, it simply feels a lot less like the traditional definition of work. I've also found that travel inspires in a way that few other things can. I now work in a media and marketing universe, where I'm paid to understand how communication impacts people and the decisions they make. It's tough to be great at a role like that when you're around the same type of people from the same type of place each day. When you subject yourself to different cultures, your biases and

5. REMOTE TRANSITION

If you're presently employed in what I'd describe as a "normal" job – one that involves a daily commute and requires you, even if unofficially, to be at a given place from a certain hour to a certain hour – you probably have some sort of routine. Your alarm goes off at some infuriating hour, a magical hand forces you into the shower, you begrudgingly climb into clothing that's entirely too uncomfortable for 5:19AM, and you force a smile as you grab something unhealthy for breakfast and casually acknowledge that there's no way you'll be getting to the gym today.

I exaggerate, of course, but that description isn't as uncommon as we all wish it were. Early on in my career, that was me. Occasionally, anyway. Due to unwritten rules of corporate politics, I felt that I had to show my face in the office at least a couple of times per week, even with a role that could be completed from anywhere. I was young, I was exceedingly appreciative for the opportunity, and I was actually quite thrilled with only having to trek 3 hours round-trip to the office every *other* day.

It was during those maddening commutes – chock full of peril – that I began to realize the true value of time. For the average worker required to put in eight full hours, living 1.5 hours away from work translates into an 11 hour workday. And that's if traffic cooperates. Extrapolate that over the course of a month, a year, or even a that you could be seen with everyone else being seen in a nondescript building? So that you could punch in and stare at your laptop for eight hours over there, instead of over here? Maybe it's worth it to you, but for me, it definitely is not. In fact, every telecommuter I've spoken to about it feels similarly: those who are able to work from anywhere are tremendously aware of the hours that they're retaining

In my case, I reasoned that I could switch to a work-from-over the course of each week — and still have more time for myself

for me, a win for my employer, and a great way to accomplish more

prodigious proportions. These newfound hours could also be poured

I realize that not everyone can simply reach into dusty chainmail armor suit, rub mud on their face, and storm out of their current role. This is real life, and you (probably) aren't Russell Crowe from *Gladiator*. But even if you're trapped in a routine that forces you into an office each day, there are steps that can be taken to slowly work your way out of the system. It most certainly was not an overnight switch for me, but by embracing a remote transition, I was able to make the most of a traditional office job while preparing myself for a fully remote role to come.

STEP 1: PREPARE FOR MORE

There's no need to sugarcoat it: if you're looking to get more time back from The Man, and acquire more freedom by being in the office less, you best be prepared to work for it. It seems counterintuitive, I know. It feels as if you're letting the system win. It feels as if you're being forced to pay a penalty for something that should already be rightfully yours. But trust me on this: it's not a battle worth fighting.

Consider the bigger picture. If you were hired to fill an office role, and all of your colleagues are enduring the same commute that you are, it's reasonable to assume that you're going to have to pony up a little extra if you're ever to be granted special consideration as it applies to showing up. My hope is that within a decade, once telecommuting's stigma fades in the way that it has with online degrees, what's presently the exception will become the norm. But until that point, you have to recognize that an arrangement whereby you only come into the office once, twice, or thrice weekly is going to strike others in one of two ways: as an injustice, or as an opportunity. For folks in the former camp, they're unlikely to be determined enough to realize that they too could be functional outside of the office, and will instead resort to rolling their eyes. For folks in the latter camp – well, those are the folks you want to band together with. Those are your go-getters. Those are the folks with enough wherewithal to understand the balance of give-and-take in the workplace.

In the earliest days of my working career, I was a Supply Chain Analyst for Nortel – a fanciful title for someone that managed millions of dollars of aging parts on a variety of Excel spreadsheets. It was obvious early on that my workday consisted of me manipulating a computer program for eight hours, addressing over-the-cubical-wall questions that could have easily been delivered over email or via an instant messaging program, and addressing calls from all over the globe that could – you guessed it – be theoretically answered from anywhere.

The role was challenging, but not overbearing. I never had to pull an all-nighter to meet my objectives, but I also realized that my physical presence in the office was of little consequence. To boot, Nortel was (at the time) a world leader in the VoIP space, even going so far as to equip my work laptop with a "soft phone" that enabled along with another 4 to 6 in miscellaneous "getting ready" hours. The actual dollar savings that go along with fewer miles on your vehicle, fewer stops at the pump, or fewer reloads on your subway card should be the ultimate cherry on top. Mentally, all of that was worth a lot to me, and it should be to you as well. If you're giddy just thinking about reclaiming those hours and dollars, the thought of having to exert extra effort to make yourself more invaluable to your employer shouldn't frighten you. In fact, what you're doing is using this as motivation to be even better at your job — something we should all aspire to, anyway.

STEP 2: PICK YOUR TARGETS

So, you're as mentally stimulated as LeBron James prior to Game 7 of the NBA Finals. Or, for those with no reference to sports whatsoever, you're as hyped as a third grader on Christmas morning. Let's just agree that your mind is in the right place to do what it takes to earn yourself some time outside of the office, cool? Cool.

The next step is going to be to identify variables that would justify a few days working from home (or anywhere, really). Wh about? What frustrations seem to crop up time and time again, seemingly due to no one in the workplace choosing to own it? What goals does your division or business have that aren't being met because everyone claims to have workloads that are maxed out? What ambitions do you have for your slice of the business? Are there areas where you know you could improve things for everyone if you just decided to chart a course and make it happen? Said another way: what can you do for your manager, yourself, your colleagues, and your employer as a whole that you aren't presently required to do?

Even if you're currently in a position that has you doing far too much, not all hope is lost. For starters, you'll be gaining additional hours and energy if allowed to stop the commute. Secondly, you may be able to redirect your efforts on lower-hanging fruit, or projects that'll end up having a much more defined impact on your workplace. Rarely does the phrase "I don't have time!" ring true. In my experience, people make time for what they want. People *have* time for things they care about. People *make* time for tasks that they view as essential. For some, it'll be about redirecting their work efforts away from tasks that aren't making a difference, and instead embracing projects that can lead to real change.

STEP 3: THE CONVERSATION

In life, preparation is everything. So, it stands to reason that the same is true in the workplace. Before scheduling a half-hour with your manager, you need to have a solid (albeit highly flexible) plan. Before approaching the powers that be on an alternative work schedule, you should be prepared to show that you've done your due diligence. Your case should leave no doubt that you've thought everything through, and that you're requesting this change not to benefit you, but to benefit the workplace. (It goes without saying, but this point should actually be true – any manager worth his or her salt will see straight through a veiled attempt to spend less time in the office for reasons that are entirely self-serving.)

I'd suggest a three-pronged approach. The first prong involves an admission that you're requesting consideration for a schedule that enables out-of-office work for a certain amount of days per week. Conventional wisdom would suggest that you save this nugget for last – *after* you've told your manager all of these amazing things you're case on a couple of high-value areas that you would be excited to work on. Don't get crazy here. Rattling off a list of 18 different areas and hoping that your manager will take the time to pick and choose for you is a losing strategy. Do your own homework and determine which areas are most vital to the company, and that you'd be best equipped to help out with. Moreover, make clear that your suggestions are based on your own research of pain points around the organization, but if your manager has items that he or she has secretly been on the hunt for someone to tackle, you'd be more than willing to take responsibility.

The final prong is admitting that you're only looking for a trial period, and that you aren't expecting an indefinite change. To best understand this, attempt to place yourself in the shoes of your manager. If you're working in a very conservative environment, realize that the manager is going to instantly worry about potential backlash from other direct reports should he or she grant your wish. It's on *you* to provide the ammunition necessary to answer those inquiries. If your manager can address any incoming complaints by pointing out additional (or more important) tasks that you're taking on in exchange for flexibility, that's great for you. If your manager can explain that your two days per week outside of the office will be used to better your health, that's great for you. Without this ammunition, the (sad) assumption is that you're simply finagling for extra time off. The good news here is that it's not difficult to put the kibosh on that kind of ridiculousness, so long as you're actually willing to take on meaningful tasks for the business.

If you're working in an environment where alternative work schedules are already embraced, you'll have a much easier time. But, if you're acting as a pioneer, you'll need to provide more justification than would seem reasonable. That said, being a pioneer is an opportunity to prove that workers of all stripes can be as effective, if not more so, when given flexibility on when and where they work.

Entering into a half-hour meeting with the expectation of having your schedule changed forever is foolish, hence my suggestion to make clear that you're willing to revert back to a traditional schedule if the manager feels that it's just not working out. (*Psst... if you're dedicated and passionate, this will never actually happen.*) Still, it's vital to provide an exit strategy to your manager. If they have nothing to lose, but plenty of potential gains, it becomes much easier to agree to an alternative work schedule. You're effectively building in a layer of accountability, and are agreeing up front to allow your manager to revoke this added flexibility at any time should it become necessary. That's a great feeling to have as a manager, and yours will be appreciative that you're aware of their challenges, too.

The added benefit of this is that it opens up yet another door for communication with your manager. It gives you even more time to discuss what's working, what isn't, and what opportunities you're seeing. It provides more time for talking about actual life, enabling a better relationship with someone that (should) matter very much to you. It also paves the way for you to eventually transition to a fully remote role, and it opens up the possibility for an actual work-from-anywhere process to be implemented at your company. If you're the guy or gal who forges the path for alternative work schedules in your organization, you may just have a statue of yourself erected outside of your company's home office. A statue that you'll never be required to show up and see, of course, but it's the thought that counts.

STEP 4: SET CHECKPOINTS

Checkpoints for you are just as important as checkpoints with your manager. If you reach a point where you aren't strolling into the office very often, the lines between life and work begin to fade. Eventually, if you find a fully remote role, they'll vanish entirely. That's frightening for some, but it's a fear that's easily addressed. My suggestion is to use your favorite reminder or calendaring program to ping you once per quarter. Within that reminder should be a few questions:

1. Are you maintaining connections with your manager and your colleagues?
2. Are you reaching or exceeding your work goals, despite being out of the office?
3. Are you at a point where you could request even more time away from the office? If not, what needs to happen in the next three months to change this answer to 'Yes'?

Given that I've been fortunate enough to transition into a fully remote role, that third question no longer applies to my situation. But if you aren't quite there yet, that third question should serve as motivation to reach a point where you can delete it. These recurring gut checks are equally recommended for those in an office setting, but I find them particularly vital for work-from-anywhere employees.

If you're reading this book, there's a high likelihood that you posses an innate level of motivation and focus that would allow you to operate at a high level regardless of location. But for many, the idea of working from anywhere other than a gray cubicle is daunting – terrifying, even. I'm convinced that anyone (yes, even you!) can muster the will to maintain focus from anywhere, but if you don't keep yourself in check, one of two things will happen. Either you'll never advance beyond where you are, preventing you from being able to justify an even more flexible schedule, or your work progress will slip and your manager will regret ever cutting you loose. At home, on the road, or sitting behind a desk over the sea in French Polynesia, no one is going to keep tabs on your daily progress. For remote workers, that responsibility falls squarely on the worker. Even for the most diligent, routine checkpoints make it easier to keep yourself honest.

STEP 5: BE ON THE LOOKOUT

Once you've had a taste of life on the other side of the office, it's practically impossible to go back. When I consider a job offer, the ability to work from wherever I want is a form of currency. There's base salary, benefits, vacation time, and the ability to work from anywhere. For an employer, that's one extra factor to play with when providing an offer of total compensation that isn't entirely reliant on a dollar amount. For an employee, it's the realization that time and flexibility are just as important as money once you reach a certain point.

To that end, being able to concretely list examples of projects you've managed, savings you've delivered, sales you've made, and initiatives you've launched **while working remotely** makes your resume a lot more impressive. Telling a prospective employer that you're able to accomplish anything while working from anywhere is one thing; tossing them a resume that proves it is something else entirely.

While there's something to be said about staying put and working towards a fully remote role within the organization that you're presently in, any employee brimming with ambition should be on the lookout for a role that's more suited to being accomplished remotely. If you aren't keeping an eye on your contacts and the overall job market for your particular skill set, you're missing out on opportunities. Once you've proven that you can indeed accomplish meaningful tasks remotely, you can then pitch your skills to a new subset of potential employers.

Don't get me wrong – I'm all about loyalty. I spent over seven years at *Engadget*, and swore up and down that I'd never leave on my own accord. Of course, that was the first fully remote role that I ever fell into, and I felt that I owed it all of my effort for thoroughly changing my life. But prior to *Engadget*, I worked at Nortel in a partially remote role. Everything was rosy, until it wasn't. In early 2009, Nortel filed for bankruptcy. A couple of weeks later, I was invited into an uninviting room where I was told that my job – along with the roles of many others – was being dissolved. Mercifully, I had begun a freelance writing role at *Engadget* back in 2006, and was able to transition into a full-time role shortly after Nortel crumbled into

LinkedIn contacts and see where people have transitioned to. Consult with yourself and see if there's a role or a company that

available. Keep a pulse on

and what they're working on.

your mailbox. They're hidden between the lines, hinted at within conversation threads on Twitter, and occasionally, behind the suggestion that's on the tip of your tongue. If you're saving yourself time by working remotely, don't be afraid to see what other roles are out there – even if they're freelance or part-time. I'm only 30, but the two most meaningful roles in my short career began as freelance gigs where location mattered not. The rest was up to me, as it can be for you.

STEP 6: CONSIDER ENTREPRENEURSHIP

I won't go into great detail on what it takes to strike out on your own and become your own boss -- there are plenty of guides already available that cover precisely that. I will say, however, that owning your own revenue stream is a great way to start a remote career. It's daunting, less flexible, and typically annihilates the notion of "time off," but it *does* provide ultimate freedom in regard to your whereabouts. It's not unusual for remote employees who are engaged with a proper employer to start side businesses in unrelated fields – fields that they're particularly passionate about. If the proper stars align, it's possible for those side hustles to become one's primary focus. Remote workers tend to be ambitious, so this progression is a logical one.

If you're running into an endless series of brick walls in an attempt to transition to a remote role within your current organization, consider entrepreneurship. It won't be as kind to your sleep schedule from the outset, as you'll likely be either chained to your computer or at the whim of your initial clients, but the long-term horizon is bright. Starting a business with the objective of being remote gives you plenty of motivation to push through the tough, early days, knowing that you'll earn more flexibility should you succeed.

One unmistakable perk of this arrangement is the talent pool you'll have at your disposal. Should your venture become large enough to warrant additional employees, you'll be able to hire the world's greatest – regardless of location. If the thought of hiring top performers from a truly global stack of resumes excites you, you've already put yourself in the proper mindset to run a remote business.

and he found a fair amount of flexibility in it. Wherever he went, he'd brighten the day of everyone in his path. He savored the simple things in life — grabbing a fried bologna sandwich and watching the Harleys cruise by during Bike Week in Myrtle Beach. When people asked him what he did, he didn't respond with his occupation. He told them *what he was*: he was a fun-loving husband, a traveler, and a sucker for southern cooking. Like I said, all figured out.

As a society, we're conditioned to let our occupation define us. When we meet a stranger for the first time, it's natural to wonder what they work on. I get it — your job is probably what consumes you more than anything else, but it shouldn't be what *defines* you. If you don't take matters into your own hands, this planet will have you living to work. The goal should be just the opposite — working to live.

I've found that purpose is largely tied to relationships. If you're a surgeon saving lives on a daily basis, perhaps you've no desire to spend less time in the operating room. If you're a coach responsible for steering at-risk youth away from a life of crime, you may want nothing more than to spend all of your available hours at work. Some roles, however, aren't as satisfying. For many, work stands as an obstacle that prevents a more meaningful relationship with friends and family. For others, it restricts a burning desire to see the world. While everyone's inner yearnings are different, I'd argue that we're all looking to find work that's gratifying, or at least an *approach* to work that allows us to find gratification elsewhere.

Remote roles are uniquely engineered to enable precisely that. By their nature, they take place wherever you're most comfortable. For some, it's a home office. For others, it's a coworking space. For me, it changes constantly – sometimes there's no place like rural North Carolina, but if there's a desk and an Internet connection, I'll work from anywhere. Because really, why not?

Too often, people are only remembered after they pass away. It's unfortunate in every fathomable way. A person works their life away, fixated on the next task at hand, only to slip away from this Earth and never enjoy the legacy that they leave behind. Don't get me wrong – living your life in a way that will make others remember you fondly is exactly what I'd recommend doing. But I'd wager that crafting a legacy that's alive every single day trumps all, and it's tough to do that if you're squandering chunks of it commuting to a place that isn't emboldening you in some way.

The hard truth is that the commuting class doesn't receive too many opportunities to really enjoy life outside of work. Do you honestly think you can enjoy all that life has to offer with two weeks of vacation and a fistful of government holidays? Do you really want to grow old inside a cubical? Are you really trying to set a record for most hours commuted?

My world view changed dramatically when I was able to work remotely on a full-time basis. Once Nortel left me behind and *Engadget* became my daily focus, I clocked more hours than I'd ever imagined. I worked days, afternoons, evenings, nights, weekends, and holidays. I had fallen into a job that allowed me to express my passions, and those hours didn't feel like work at all. I found a job that I was proud to infuse into my legacy. I was *Engadget*, and it was me. Not everyone will be so fortunate, of course, but it's worth hunting for a role that truly aligns with your skills. A role that suits you is apt to fuel your passions, enabling you to accomplish two things in parallel: build your legacy at work, and build your legacy elsewhere.

Finding a role that enables such a parallel provides a renewed sense of purpose, and in my case, made me aware of the impact I was having on others. If you're approaching your job in a way that seeks to improve the lives of your colleagues, you're living your legacy. In doing so, you'll also make time for improving the lives of others outside of work. For me, that's traveling with my wife, friends, and family. For others, it's volunteering, or jamming in a garage with a few close knuckleheads, or writing scripts for movies that might just make it to Sundance. Even if your present situation doesn't allow much time for travel, having excess hours to strengthen relationships with your spouse, your youngsters, and your neighbors is a powerful motivator.

body is unchained from a physical location, you're free to make an impact like never before. When you can work from anywhere, you can easily transition from work to life. When my workday is done, I take two steps from a chair and I'm instantly alive. My commute is **two steps**. Over the course of a year, the amount of hours that I'm allowed to live simply because I don't have a commute is staggering. I love the work that I do, but even on tough days, a downtrodden soul is always just two steps away from being revived.

Great managers will recognize that one's best work emerges when the employee is in an ideal place mentally. Some of my most creative ideas have come while drenched in sweat along a hiking trail, or while sitting idly under the sun alongside my wife and dog. True creativity is best derived from a happy mind, and happy minds are rarely found within rigid confines. I'm also far healthier due to my ability to work from anywhere. I rarely have an excuse to skip a workout – after all, the hour I'll spend bettering my condition is the same hour I'm *not* spending on a commute.

I'm not trying to get all theological on you, but the soul wasn't meant to be ruled by work. The soul was meant to roam, to enjoy the company of others, to adore the beauty of nature. Work is simply a means to those ends, and it's easier to keep that in mind when you're able to toil from a place of your choosing. If your legacy feels dead, or is being wholly defined by the stipulations of your job, it's time to seek something better for yourself. Trust me when I say that you aren't alone; I've worked with a number of teams that all left various roles in search of one that allowed them to simply **live more**. When you find a job that enables you to feel alive, and imposes no restrictions on where you perform, you'll give it everything you've got (and then some).

7. NECESSARY EQUIPMENT

Given that a conventional office job most certainly isn't for me, it's reasonable to assume that a remote role may not suit everyone. If you're going to embrace it, you're going to need a very different toolkit than most every other worker on the planet. Oddball stuff, but stuff that makes you faster, more productive, and more nimble all the while. I've spent the better part of my career honing what I use on a daily basis, and while mental workflows are critical, there's no denying that one's arsenal of gadgetry plays a big role.

Throughout this chapter, I'll outline the tools I view as essential, along with justification and use-case scenarios. Some of them require money to procure; others, patience and a little luck. Without further ado…

#1: A MOBILE INTERNET HOTSPOT FROM VERIZON

Cellular infrastructure contributes more to my ability to remain highly productive from anywhere than anything else. It's impossible to pin down, but I'd wager that at least 20 percent of the articles that led to my eventual world record were uploaded and published over a mobile network. Admittedly, I'm fortunate to reside in the United States, where mobile networks are advanced, and dangerously close to ubiquitous. That being said, I've found that wireless networks are generally more accessible and more reliable than wireline networks when traveling overseas.

If you're a resident of the U.S., I've no hesitation in recommending a mobile hotspot from Verizon Wireless. Its 4G LTE network is the broadest of any carrier in the country, which means that you'll find exceptionally fast Internet speeds in the most random of places. Which is great, because America's most beautiful locales are typically in the most random of places. Great employers will either buy one for you or reimburse you, but even if they won't, the ~$50 to $60 per month you'll pay for a healthy chunk of mobile data is well worth it. 4G LTE is fast enough to be used as a home Internet replacement, but current data caps prevent that from being feasible. My guess is that folks who pick this book up in a bargain bin circa 2029 will have quite the chuckle at the above statement. Eventually, wireless bandwidth won't be a concern, but it is for now.

So, what does $50 per month get you? A battery-operated puck that connects to a mobile network and allows anything with a Wi-Fi radio to get online. That's mighty powerful. I've been in airports, riding shotgun in an Impala, and high atop mountains when I've needed to get something done. With a hotspot, my laptop – which I'll address in a minute, pinky promise! – is able to get online and plow through work so long as there's a mobile signal in the vicinity.

#2: A CAPACIOUS IPHONE FROM AT&T

Yeah, you'd save money by bundling a smartphone purchase with a mobile hotspot purchase at Verizon, but you shouldn't do that. It's actually one of the few times I'd recommend *not* saving money. Here's why. First off – and I'll warn you, this is pretty nerdy – Verizon's native network does not offer free calling and 4G LTE in the United States Virgin Islands. This is a big deal for two reasons: One, AT&T treats the United States Virgin Islands just like Oregon or New Hampshire, which is to say that there are no roaming fees when traveling there. Second, I would never encourage you to make any decision in life that would hamper, prevent, or even discourage you from spending time in the United States Virgin Islands. It's an exceptional place and you should go there immediately.

Now that we're square on that, here's the other reason: redundancy and variety are vital assets when you're a remote employee. If your primary method of getting online is a Verizon mobile hotspot, you're going to want a smartphone on a different network to act as your fallback connection. There are locations where Verizon is superior to AT&T, and then there are locations where AT&T is superior to Verizon. If you have devices with connections to both networks, all the better.

As for the iPhone recommendation? I've used every major operating system since the dawn of the smartphone, and while there are cases to be made for other phones, I've *never* met anyone who has switched to iPhone and hated it. It's easy to use, maintains its value quite well, and works wonderfully as a mobile hotspot. You simply visit the Settings menu and trigger the functionality, and just like that, you can share your phone's data connection with your laptop.

Finally, spring for the largest (capacity) iPhone you can afford. 128GB may seem like overkill, but it's not. Remote employees need weird stuff on their phones – stuff that normal people just won't understand. As a remote employee, you may find yourself in a foreign country with no data connection. To prepare for that, you need to download foreign language dictionaries and navigational maps of the world in offline form. Between dictionaries (Jibbigo), offline maps (Maps.me), and other offline files that help out when I'm abroad and unable to secure a connection, around 20GB of my phone is tied up.

Remote employees also take pictures – *lots* of pictures, because their scenery changes more frequently than most. Pictures take up a lot of space, and deleting pictures because you're "running out of room" is up there with "batteries not included" on the sadness meter.

#3: APPLE MACBOOK AIR

Look, Apple makes great stuff. Not flawless, mind you, but great. The MacBook Air is amongst the thinnest, lightest, and longest-lasting computers on the face of the planet. Those three things are crucial when you're continually on the move. It's light enough that I can take it hiking (hey, you never know!), and it's longevous enough to endure a flight from New York to London. As a remote employee, your laptop is everything. You can accomplish small chores on a phone or tablet, but real work happens on a computer. Make sure you get a great one.

#4: ELITE AIRLINE STATUS

Flying isn't easy. Air travel is a royal pain, fraught with volatility and unpredictable delays. It's also amazing, and you should fly as much as possible. To make things easier, do everything that you can to earn elite status with a certain airline or alliance. Usually, this means flying with the same airline or alliance religiously. Beyond the potential for upgrades, you'll be treated like a customer (versus a number) when you run into issues. You can also earn lounge status to escape the madness in the main terminal, and in general, elite status simply enables you to be more productive and less stressed when you're at the airport and in the air. There's just no getting around it: VIP treatment makes work and leisure travel a lot more tolerable.

ACCESSORIES AND DOODADS

Below, you'll find a list of killer items that don't demand a long explanation. They're just wonderful, plain and simple. Google these to learn more or buy them.

1. **Targus World Power Travel Adapter:** It's tiny, lightweight, and adapts to every major power outlet in the world except for Australia. (Pick up a dedicated Aussie adapter if you're routinely heading Down Under.)
2. **Monster 4-port Outlets To Go:** A compact, highly mobile 4-port power strip that enables a single foreign power outlet to charge four U.S. devices. Moreover, it gives you hero status in an airport when there's legions of people trying to take advantage of the single plug over by Gate B42.
3. **Catalyst waterproof smartphone case:** This company makes the lightest, sleekest, most functional cases on the market. It also gives you a reason to capture HD footage of yourself swimming around with sea turtles in Kauai.
4. **Google Drive:** The best free cloud storage system. I don't store anything on my Mac directly; it's all on Google Drive. I trust that my stuff will be safe there, and you should do the same.
5. **Clip Menu:** A simplistic, free Mac utility that keeps an insanely long log of everything you've copied-and-pasted. Great for saving your bacon during a computer crash.
6. **Mountain Hardware Agama pack:** The best way to carry

everything. It's light, deceptively huge, great for hiking, and well designed. It's a secret weapon for those who prefer to fly light, as you can fit a week's worth of clothing in here and it'll still slip underneath the seat in front of you.

7. **Passport:** Goes without saying. If you aren't breaking out your passport on an annual basis, reevaluate everything.

8. **BlueRigger aux audio cable:** Plopping down in a rental car? Great. Realizing that you have no way to stream music from your phone? Soul-crushing.

9. **KnowRoaming SIM sticker:** The issue of global roaming is a pet peeve of mine, and while this solution won't work for every country, it's a great way to save money on voice and data for many of the most frequently visited ones.

10. **KeepGo:** For nations that aren't included in KnowRoaming's unlimited plan, KeepGo will send you a SIM or a mobile hotspot to cover the nation(s) that you're heading to. It's pricier, but usually beats hunting down a local SIM card upon arrival.

In general, I'd advise to operate with as little as possible. Minimalism is a trait worth embracing for remote employees. The less you carry, the easier it is to accept where serendipitous winds may take you. There's no doubt that working remotely – particularly on the road – requires adaptation to operating on a small computer. At home, you can lean on external displays, a keyboard, and a mouse to make things a bit easier, but it's worth putting in the effort to learn the computer that you own.

Everyone has workflows that apply uniquely to them, and while it's difficult to pinpoint how or why I do everything that I do on my computer, I'll offer one closing piece of advice: learn to love keyboard shortcuts. If you're able to replace mousing about with a keyboard command, you'll save a little time. And in a week, that'll amount to a lot of time.

8. FINANCIAL SIDE EFFECTS

You'd have to triple my salary to get me to do the same thing I do each day, but from an office in a big city. That probably sounds like a gross exaggeration, but it's not. Anyone who has tasted the freedom and flexibility of working remotely understands what I mean – it's almost impossible to put a price on what it'd take to get you to go back to the office. There's a price, of course, but it's the kind of price that's so high, I'd question your business' priorities if you actually offered it to me. That's how much I value being able to work from anywhere, and if you're able to secure a remote role for yourself, you'll discover quite a few similar financial oddities.

My first remote role didn't pay very well, but it was well worth taking. Everyone values time and freedom differently, but you actually can begin to put some boundaries on what a remote role could be worth to you.

- Calculate how many hours per week you spend commuting, and multiply that out for a full year's worth of back-and-forth. Multiple *that* by what you're getting paid per hour, and the figure will probably surprise you. Time is money. Time is opportunity. Time is *life*.

- To get even more specific, add up what you're paying in fuel, maintenance costs to your vehicle, and/or metro fees for those fortunate enough to live close to a reliable public transit system. Now, envision that dropping to $0.00. Suddenly, it becomes obvious that you could work for a lot less in a remote role and procure just as much value.

- Another factor to consider is home office expenses. I'll let you and your accountant work out the particulars, but those who carve out sections of their abode dedicated to work can save a bit come tax time, too.
- Then, there's the issue of food. Office dwellers frequently scoot out for lunch, spending large sums in the process. Those who control their work environment are able to keep more groceries on hand and prepare their own meals – meals built from ingredients they choose. If you care at all about your health, there's something to be said about having this kind of freedom, and you'll probably save money all the while.
- Given that I'm home on a regular basis, my home is my gym. I have flexibility when it comes to choosing the time that I work out each day, and I'm saving money on a trip to the gym, a membership to the gym, and all of that fancy clothing that gyms coerce you to wear.
- Being able to knock out errands during business hours is a major plus for your finances. You spend less fuel and time waiting in rush hour traffic, and you're able to get things done on a weekday instead of paying whatever you're asked after-hours or on a weekend.

With all of that being said, you should certainly do the math if you're offered a remote role that pays less on the surface. When everything's computed, the offers may balance out more than you expect. And, if you're able to maintain your pay at a new remote role, or transition from the office to your home… well, it's pretty exciting to stash that extra fundage away for the future.

Conversely, you're in a better position to command *more* in a remote role due to the efficiencies gained. Removing the commute, politicking, and mindless meetings enables you to have a whole lot more time for – you know – working. It's not unreasonable to think that a dedicated remote worker couldn't accomplish the work of two folks in an office. I'd like to think that I'm living proof of that. From an employer's point of view, there's potential to lower your overall salary costs *and* pay each person on the payroll more by employing a remote team. Lower costs *and* happier, wealthier employees? That kind of combination is hard to find with any other arrangement.

While operating as Managing Editor at *Engadget*, I wore a slew of hats, and did so from all corners of the globe. I aided in remotely training each new writer we hired, penned hundreds of articles per month, handled HR questions, appeared on radio and television programs to bolster our brand, interfaced with our design staff, and generally put out fires that arose from California to London and everywhere in between. My view is that my employer gained massively by having a single individual that was intimately familiar with all of those things, and it also saved the company money by not having to hire a handful of people to juggle what I was juggling. I put in well over 40 hours per week, of course, but between my paycheck and the ability to operate from anywhere, I felt I was fairly compensated for that.

If you're an employer toying with the idea of implementing a remote team, I'd encourage you to do it. Not only can you save money by paying a smaller team more, but you'll attract top-tier talent willing to go the extra mile in exchange for added flexibility.

9. DON'T BE A JERK

It sounds obvious... too obvious, really. So obvious that you may pick this chapter as the one that you're going to casually skip. Please, don't. I've learned that much is given in life to those who simply master the obvious. Showing up on time (or early), being known as "reliable" throughout your network, and volunteering to dominate tasks that clearly aren't designated to be your burden. Most sane people would agree that those are traits we see in ourselves, but let's get really real with each other: is that how everyone else sees you, or how *you* see you?

I grew up not wanting for anything, but it wasn't because I was birthed into the Trump family. My mother spent her youth toiling on a farm, forced by her own circumstances to work so much that she oftentimes neglected school. My father was raised alongside legions of siblings – so many that I've honestly lost count, but enough that it made it pretty hard to spoil any single one of them. I attended a middle school and high school that a great many parents would turn their nose up at. A rough neighborhood, kids who largely couldn't care less about learning, and teachers who weren't compensated enough to change the culture.

Despite having ample opportunities to enjoy my youth with drugs and alcohol, I abstained. My summers were spent on a potato farm, doing this and that and coming home covered – literally head to toe – in filth. Needless to say, I worked entirely too hard for my money to spend it on such frivolous vices, and it didn't hurt that I was raised in a loving, accepting home with Christian values.

The point here is that I wasn't embedded into a path that would necessarily lead to success. It certainly wasn't a path that I believed would lead to greater-than-average freedom. My mother maintained that a few essentials, however, would give me more opportunity than anything else: kindness, timeliness, and a dependable nature. You know, the same traits that Eagle Scouts – *Troop 383, holler at your boy!* – have sworn to live by.

There were days when she'd come home from a long day spent at a local paper plant, saddened by treatment she'd been dealt by one person or another. Some of the stories were infuriating. "Get out of there!," I'd say. "Don't give those folks an ounce of extra energy!" She handled things differently, though. "Kill 'em with kindness," she'd say, forcing a smile that quickly became authentic. "Man," I thought, "that takes some grit."

In life, it's far easier to react with vitriol and violence than to take the higher road. Particularly so when you aren't sure if anyone around you will ever appreciate your choice to hold back and persevere. What I can tell you is this: you won't ever wreck your career by taking the high road, and in some strange way, it'll always work out to your benefit. It may take some time – years, even – but it'll come back around.

I can't even begin to count the hundreds and thousands of individuals I've met in my working career. Marketers, writers, videographers, analysts, editors, lovers, haters, cyclists, daredevils, a man named Tim Stevens[8] who transcends all positive adjectives, and aimless wanderers. In many cases, running into someone here or there for a few minutes doesn't seem like a big deal. But the impression you can leave on someone within only a few moments is staggering.

I ran into a guy that was considering starting his own company one year at CES, a giant electronics show in Las Vegas where over 150,000 people come together to nerd out. I didn't know this gentleman, and he only knew me tangentially from my years at *Engadget*. We chatted for five, maybe eight minutes about the struggles he'd probably have, and I rattled off a few tips that came to mind before being ushered away to whatever else I was scheduled to do. "Good luck!" was the last thing I actually recall saying.

---

[8]Stevens, Tim. *Twitter.*<https://twitter.com/tim_stevens>

Almost a year later, he emailed me. Things were swell, and he wanted to know if I could talk shop about what his company was planning next. A lot had transpired in the year between our two points of contact, but our conversation picked up as if we hadn't missed a beat. I realize that this is just one example – in fact, I've uttered "Good luck!" to a lot of people at CES that have yet to call me back – but it's proof to me that being kind pays off. Taking time for someone else pays off. Bending a schedule to meet someone that thinks they admire you pays off. Maybe not even monetarily, but as I've argued throughout this book, compensation takes many forms.

Choosing to take the high road in the face of conflict, adversity, and uncertainty is not nearly as easy as it sounds, but particularly for remote employees, it's vital. When you're in a role that prevents you from having the same amount of "face time" with your manager or peers as everyone else, you're at a disadvantage. You won't be given the benefit of the doubt if your character or personality comes into question, so it's critical to make the encounters you do have ones that shine. Learning how to express positivity and humor over lifeless mediums such as email and IM will enable you to go far. In a remote role, your smile won't compensate for anything. It's on you to figure out how to still seem human to everyone else that you work with, and it starts by not being a jerk.

There's no question that having *some* writing ability comes in handy here. I'm a proponent of conversational writing, and I use that when I communicate with my colleagues over email, IM, text, etc. Write to people as if you're talking to them.

It doesn't hurt that I see my colleagues in person every other month or so, and I make an effort to not be a hermit. Remember: I love to travel, and I love to *visit* the office. But there's a monumental difference between visiting and being chained.

I'm convinced that being exceptionally kind has two other benefits: it makes you a happier human, and it enables further gains in productivity. Nicer people, by their nature, end up with more on their plate. Everyone has limits – and I'd encourage you to be mindful of yours – but readily accepting additional responsibility is a great way to prove that you're cut out for handling work remotely. It's impressive to see someone grab something by the horns without a mandate, and you'll be helping both yourself and your colleagues by doing so. To boot, those who remain fixated on issues are rarely the type that you'd love to take to Disneyland. Motivated people are happy people. You can look at added responsibility in two ways: 1) *Ugh* or 2) *I got this.* (I'd advise the second option whenever feasible.)

I strive to stifle my inner jerk and be a positive person. (If you're reading this book and you can cite a specific case where the aforementioned assumption is comically wrong, please ping me privately. I owe you an apology, a hug, and a Cook-out milkshake.) It's important to point out that I'm not advocating for being someone you aren't; I'm suggesting that you place a high priority on character if you're going to be "out of sight" to much of the workplace. Fair or not, expectations for remote workers are a little different. In the case of personality, however, it's a great excuse to get bent back into shape.

10. WHAT COULD POSSIBLY GO WRONG?

I'd be remiss of my duties as an honest gentleman if I didn't address the downsides to working remotely, of which there are many. I wouldn't be writing this book with such joviality if I didn't think that the pros outweighed the cons, but I still want to provide a critical look at the other side of the coin.

Remote work is most definitely not for everyone. For some, their passions are situated in areas where working remotely just isn't advantageous. If you're gunning to become the President of the United States, you darn well better be alright with residing in Washington, D.C. If you're in a place where remote work might be an option, however, I owe it to you to showcase some of the pitfalls that I've encountered over the years.

THERE IS NO WORK/LIFE BALANCE

I'm just going to throw it out there: those looking for well-defined lines between work and leisure should stay where they are. My view here is that the work/life balance is being obliterated everywhere, both remotely and in the office, which is why I'd rather work on my own turf. But to be a great remote worker – particularly one that truly takes advantage of being able to work *anywhere* – you're going to have to prioritize work over yourself at times.

I've found that remote work generally embraces a work/life *extreme*. At times, it's extremely enjoyable, enabling me to pet a dolphin and take a dip in the ocean during the day while churning through tasks in the evening. At times, it's extremely... well, extreme. Fire drills can occur while everyone else is on the subway headed home, and it'll be on you to implement a solution. Occasionally, vacations can be interrupted by a jarring email – even if it's something you *can* ignore, great workers won't have an easy time purging it from their memory.

My own family would tell that I was almost completely absent from holiday gatherings for a number of years, despite my person being there. I'd look up and smile, greet someone, and then immediately refocus my attention on an alarming text or email from work. It's entirely possible to be driven into addiction for fear of your remote role vanishing. It's downright horrifying for me – even now – to consider the hit I'd take from a quality of life standpoint should I ever be forced to work in a non-remote situation. That fear makes it all too easy to prioritize work over family, and I know that certain relationships have suffered in prior years due to my inability to push the workplace aside for any length of time.

The ability to work from anywhere enables you to, in theory, *work from anywhere*. It's important to establish sensible boundaries with your manager and team, but there will be times when you're overworked and hit with untimely assignments due to what's perceived as infinite flexibility.

NEGATIVE PERCEPTION

Remote work is still unorthodox. Globally, the amount of people that telecommute is still under 10 percent, so you're bound to run into others who simply cannot comprehend how it's possible to accomplish anything without being in an office. Unfortunately, some of these individuals may work at the same company as you. I'd caution you when it comes to making your private life public. Even a seemingly innocuous photo upload to Instagram during what's perceived as "business hours" could spur negativity that you don't need. Is it worth the effort to explain that you took an hour long break from nonstop pounding to catch a great view of a mountain, and that you'll be putting in a few extra hours after the office clears out? That's on you to decide, but the answer will vary by situation.

THE BATTLE FOR A SANCTUARY

Most of society makes this distinction: if you're home, you're not at work. That's a tough one to overcome. I've been right in the middle of an extremely high priority work task when FedEx arrives with a package that needs my signature. So, I break to sign for the package, but the deliverer makes the assumption that I'm just taking the day off and have *gobs* of time to chat. Awkward.

More serious than that, however, is the perception from family. When your loved ones know that you're home, they make assumptions that aren't necessarily true. They assume that you can run an errand in the middle of the day. Which could be true on *certain* days, but the assumption is usually there *every* day. For whatever reason, it's really tough to get others to understand that your home office should be treated as a sanctuary. When you're at work, you're at work. Frank conversations upfront usually help to mitigate this, but don't be surprised if you're hit with an overwhelming amount of requests from friends and family while you're working.

BUSINESS TRAVEL

I'm one that's on a mission to go just about everywhere, so traveling for work is most certainly not a negative for me. But for others, it can be. While it's technically possible to secure a remote role where you're never required to show your face, these jobs are few and far betwixt (and typically offer little room for advancement, if I'm honest). When arranging my most recent remote role, I suggested that I travel to headquarters on a monthly or bi-monthly basis, if only to touch base with everyone and sit in on meetings that I'd otherwise dial into. In my mind, it's the least I could offer to do in exchange for all the flexibility I'm being granted.

Go ahead and prepare for travel, along with all of the headaches that come with it. Delays, cancellations, lost luggage, traffic, weird meals, uncomfortable beds, days away from your family… you get the point. Remote work is rarely a ticket to never leave home; it's a ticket that enables you to avoid a daily trek into the office. That's a distinction worth recognizing.

ACCEPTABILITY AND ADVANCEMENT

You should aim to work for a company that values production. That's easier said than done, however, and you should be aware that remote employees are generally taken less seriously and aren't heavily considered for promotions that they'd get if they showed up in the office each day.

Case in point: I was able to manage lots of insanity all across the globe remotely as *Engadget*'s Managing Editor. But I knew that the company's Editor-in-Chief needed to be in either New York or San Francisco. There was simply no avoiding it – TV cameras aren't located in rural North Carolina, so I had no shot at accomplishing that very important job requirement from afar. Of course, I never actually wanted to be Editor-in-Chief. I had all I could handle, and advancement was of no concern in that particular situation. Not everyone would've been satisfied, however, so it's vital to realize that remote roles can (and often do) have professional ceilings.

Beyond all that, remote workers have to work extra hard to earn the respect and love of their colleagues. Those who operate in remote organizations will find this far more simple, but remote employees operating within a more traditional company will need to exert additional effort to meet, understand, and relate with coworkers. If you're an extrovert that enjoys the challenge of fostering new relationships, this won't bother you in the slightest. If the mere mention of it incites fear, well… don't say I didn't warn you.

PREDICTABILITY

In early 2011, my wife and I were in London. I received an email from someone that commanded my respect, and he wanted to chat on the phone. Which is great, except that I was in London… where I can't make or receive a call without paying abhorrent roaming rates. So, I informed the unnamed gentleman that I'd be available via Skype that evening. (For those unaware, Skype is a calling tool that works so long as you have a reliable Wi-Fi signal.) Around 15 minutes prior to our scheduled call, the Wi-Fi at my hotel decided to take the rest of the evening off. This is the point in the story where most folks would concede to missing the call, and in turn, the potential to form a wonderful new relationship. Not I.

I decided to scour a nearby street for a Starbucks location, intent on borrowing a bit of Wi-Fi in order to complete the call. Finding that they had all closed up, I went to the next logical place: the Regent Street Apple Store. Predictably, they too were closed for the night, so the inner MacGyver in me sprang to life. I compressed the cells in my face by peremptorily placing my left cheek up against the glass panes of the store. Moving a bit to my left, I realized that my phone could pick up a single bar of service from the Wi-Fi routers within. Achievement unlocked.

The call came through, and while we did lose each other a time or two, the mission was accomplished. We chatted, we made plans to speak again, and we're friends to this day. Also, my DNA will forever be a part of the Regent Street Apple Store door.

While this is, admittedly, one of the zanier tales I have, it's not at all unusual. The remote worker leads an unpredictable life, and trying to accomplish something as routine as a scheduled call can cause all sorts of frustration. It's because of this that you'll learn to bake in redundancies and fallbacks as you go. When heading overseas, I wrangle no fewer than two forms of mobile connectivity before ever leaving U.S. soil. When traveling domestically, I always carry a hotspot in the event that my hotel's Wi-Fi goes down. When given the option, I'll take a 2,000 word email over a phone call.

Be aware that by working odd hours in odd places, it's going to be tough to fit into the defined schedules of everyone else back in the real world. Think of it as a game, learn to laugh before you cry, and everything else will fall into place. Eventually. Maybe.

11. SO, WHERE DO I SIGN UP?

I've convinced you to never set foot in an office again, huh? I'd be proud, but the honest truth is that the arrangement sells itself. Once you've tasted the sweet, succulent nectar of working anywhere, it's tough to imagine going back. Indeed, it's tough to even envision a number that would have you entertaining the *offer* to go back.

Remote work is not without its challenges, but if you're reading this out of frustration with your current role, you realize that it's impossible to avoid headaches entirely. I'll close by providing my two pennies on the (good) types of jobs that are most suitable for remote employment. If you're already aware of a few avenues, great. If not, it's an exciting time to be looking.

The Internet has enabled a multitude of jobs that simply did not and could not exist a score ago. It is, in so many ways, the next great workplace. The Internet is the modern day office, and I'd surmise that it's only a matter of time before a wealth of new companies are started with no intention of ever spending a cent on real estate. My good pal Brian Lam cranked up *The Wirecutter*[9], a terrific publication, back in 2011. From day one, he made clear that his company would never have a physical footprint. If you speak with the folks that work

---

[9]*The Wirecutter. <http://thewirecutter.com/>*

there, you'd realize just how tightly knit that bunch is. They're scattered here, there, and everywhere, but relationships do not require office space to thrive. Increasingly, I expect companies to go this route. It's far less expensive, it enables employees to focus solely on the business, and it puts the founder in a position to recruit the best talent the entire world has to offer.

EDITORIAL

The temptation was to put "writing" here, but that's far too narrow. While great writers are obviously primed to write and publish from anywhere, editorial specialists are as well. If you have a penchant for writing, and you have a passion, there is almost certainly a publication (or ten) that you could apply at. Beyond that, even corporations need folks who are mighty with a pen. From internal blogs to corporate memos to modern marketing, the words that shape the future can be composed from anywhere.

CODING

It's truly amazing what's possible if you understand a coding language or two. Whether your intentions are to build your own apps or become a software developer for the legions of companies that are looking, coders are well-suited to create from anywhere. To boot, software engineers are in such high demand that it'd be worth your while to *become* one. If you're looking to make a stark career pivot, consider software. (And if you need a place to learn, check out The Iron Yard[10] – great teachers, short courses, and real results.)

MARKETING

The marketer's canvas is now the Internet. It's an email newsletter template, a website, an app, a banner advertisement, or an appearance on a popular podcast. It's tough weeding through the scummy, scammy online marketing offers, but if you're currently at a real company with a real marketing department, poke around and see what they need. Chances are they need a creative mind that's fantastic

---

[10]"Welcome to The Iron Yard." *The Iron Yard.*<http://theironyard.com/>

on the phone and behind a computer screen.

YOUR OWN BUSINESS

There has never been a better time to start something new. No longer do you have to relocate to Brooklyn to start a clothing line that'll gain traction. No longer must you move to Santa Fe if you're hoping to sell the art that you create. Physical storefronts and foot traffic are no longer requirements for a business to succeed. Between Zazzle, Society6, Etsy, eBay, and the hundreds of other popularized Internet storefronts, your home is the perfect business incubator. That doesn't make the process of starting and operating a small business any easier, per se, but the Internet gives you maximum flexibility when it comes to *where* that business can be headquartered.

EDUCATION

Online degrees aren't going away. With increased enrollment comes an increased demand for teachers that are willing to manage classes around the globe, with assignments coming in at all hours of the night, and students having all sorts of other activities to juggle. I have a cousin that secured a role as a guidance counselor for a college in Arizona. For years, she showed up at the office and did her job excellently. When it came time for her family to move to Alaska, the college begged her to stay. So, she did… by logging in each day from an iMac on the outskirts of Fairbanks.

EVERYWHERE ELSE

Yeah, it's a catch-all, but hear me out. If you're currently employed at a respectable company with great colleagues and a great career path ahead of you, **see what's possible**. Sit down with your manager and see what areas of the business could use a smart, dedicated mind that just so happens to work primarily from other places. While plenty of online job postings go up each day, the *best* remote roles are going to come from places that are never advertised. In many cases, it's wise to start a role at the office, and once you're an invaluable asset, start to make the case for working remotely. Even if you change departments and stay within the same company, it's worth exploring.

If there's one thing I've learned throughout my journeys in unconventional work, it's this: you'll never hear "yes" if you don't ask.

I'll close with a word of encouragement. To someone who has been commuting to a job and doing the daily grind for years, the mere thought of breaking out and pursing something as audacious as a remote career can be intimidating. You're trying to comprehend an entirely different way of working, where timing matters less and location is rarely of consequence. To boot, you're doing so in a world where this is still (mostly) a foreign concept.

Don't let any of that deter you. Advancements in technology have utterly destroyed barriers to communication, enabling people like yourself to be seen and heard from anywhere. No longer is it impossible to enjoy life on your own terms while also accomplishing professional goals. The office is something best viewed as an *idea* — not as an immovable place.

Commit yourself to adding value to your organization, and the weight placed on *where* that value is added will diminish. If you seek first to serve your colleagues, your bosses, and your company, you'll be pleasantly surprised at what else falls into place. The remote dream is not a selfish one. It is one that benefits all who recognize its virtues, and one that creates a positive cycle of working hard to live even harder.

Godspeed, and may your journeys be blessed.

Made in the USA
Middletown, DE
03 June 2015